Editing: Jan Burgess

Design: Peter Luff
Keith Faulkner

Picture research: Michelle Masek

Photo credits: Heather Angel;
Aquila Photographics; A–Z
Botanical Collection; Frank
Blackburn, David Burns; Bruce
Coleman; Elisabeth Photo Library;
David Hosking; Eric Hosking;
Natural History Photographic
Agency; Picturepoint; Dr Fred
Slater; Thames Water; Alwyne
Wheeler; World Wildlife Fund;
Zefa

First published in Great Britain in 1982 by
Macmillan Children's Books under the series title
Macmillan Countryside Books

This edition published in 1987 by
Treasure Press
59 Grosvenor Street
London W1

© Macmillan Publishers Limited 1982

ISBN 1 85051 180 2

Printed in Austria

Endpapers: Frogs and toads are now rare in many places.

COUNTRYSIDE IN DANGER

CHRIS GRAY

TREASURE PRESS

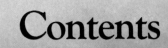

Contents

Sea and Shore

Oceans cover about three-quarters of the world's surface, and they provide the rain that all land life needs. Ocean waters contain a multitude of living things, including much of the food we eat. Sea-shores are the places where land and sea meet, where many birds breed and feed, and where we often like to go on holiday.

Both sea and shore are threatened by pollution. Nearly all the world's rubbish ends up in the sea – either dumped directly into it, or carried there by rivers. But the rubbish of our modern world – poisonous chemicals, oil, plastics, nuclear waste – is too much for the sea to absorb.

Sadly, most oil pollution is not accidental. Some ships deliberately empty their oil tanks at sea in order to clean them quickly and save time in port, even though they know that this is illegal.

An accident at sea can spill millions of litres of oil. Diving birds like guillemots get covered with it. This bird will die, because it will try to clean its feathers. The oil it swallows as it preens itself will poison it.

Puffins breed in burrows on cliffs by the sea. They only lay one egg and both parents take turns to incubate it for six weeks. Like guillemots, puffins are auks and fish under water. Many are killed unnecessarily each year by oil spillage at sea.

Land animals, including deer, sheep and otters, also feed on the shore. One oil spill at Sullom Voe in the Shetland Islands killed 3,000 birds, 200 otters and affected thousands of sheep.

Still Water

From great lakes to tiny ponds, still waters contain a host of living things. Water-loving plants grow in and around them. They are the home of fishes and crustaceans. Insects and amphibians such as frogs and newts breed in them.

There used to be many more village and farm ponds than there are now. Cars and tractors have taken over from animal power, so ponds are no longer needed to provide water for horses and cattle. Village ponds may be filled up with earth to prevent them becoming rubbish dumps. Some farmers drain ponds to tidy up their land. Farm chemicals often get into the remaining ponds and ditches. Even fertilizers from nearby fields will kill pondlife, because the chemicals used in the fertilizers are washed into ponds.

The survival of our water plants and animals may, in the end, depend on whether they can make themselves at home in new waters. While many ponds and ditches are being filled in, a few new watery habitats are being created. The big hole left once the gravel workings were complete has been flooded, and makes a pleasant place to go fishing or sailing. Places like this also make marvellous wildlife reserves, which makes them even more interesting for human visitors.

Above: Water crowfoot lives in shallow water. Its roots are embedded in the mud while its flowers stick up above the surface. There are fewer and fewer ponds for plants like it to grow. In some places, there are only half as many ponds as there were 100 years ago.

This water spider lives underwater in moorland ponds and ditches. It builds a bell-like net attached to water-plants, and carries down air bubbles to fill it.

Water spiders hunt small creatures in the pond. They carry them back to eat in their diving-bell lair. Young spiders spend the winter in old, air-filled snail shells.

Amphibians spend much of their lives on land. Toads only come to water to breed, and frogs spend more time near the water than actually in it. But they all have to lay their eggs in water. Tadpoles have gills for breathing, just like fish. They need fresh, clean water if they are to grow into adults. Frogs and toads used to be common. Their loud croaking during the springtime mating season was once a familiar sound. Today it is rarely heard for their breeding ponds are being drained.

Running Water

Kingfisher

Rivers and streams carry fresh water from mountain tops to the sea. Running water contains thousands of places for a great variety of plants and animals, from fast, cold streams, to slow, muddy rivers. It is no accident that the great and ancient cities of the world are built beside rivers. Water is a necessity of life, so people naturally settled near it. In the past, cities on rivers became rich through the trade that came in ships. The cities grew bigger, and more people meant more rubbish. Now, Europe's larger rivers are so badly polluted that practically nothing can live in them for miles downstream of a big city. Factories use river water to cool machinery, and they add to the pollution by dumping their waste matter into the water.

Even in the country, farm chemicals are carried into running water by rain as it soaks through the soil. For good drainage, farmers keep ditches and streams clear of plants so the water runs away freely. But without plants, nothing can grow. Many places that were once teeming with life are now bare and dead.

Zander

There is nothing wrong with a factory 'borrowing' water from a river, unless the factory puts back more than it takes out. This factory is plainly putting more waste into the river than it can disperse. Heat or wastes such as detergents or chemicals do great harm.

Mallard ducks

Water vole

Thoughtless fishermen sometimes cause great harm to wildlife. Every year, many animals and birds die a horrible death, trapped, strangled or wounded by old fishing-lines.

Swans dredge in the mud for grit. Accidentally, they swallow lead pellets from shotguns, and fishing weights left by careless anglers. The result is that many swans die from lead poisoning.

Algae

Otter

Meadowsweet

Wetlands

There are three main kinds of wetlands. In places like the fens, reeds, sedges and a tremendous range of other plants and animals grow. The wet areas of moors are acid bogs. They support a different kind of life, including certain strange plants which grow nowhere else. Saltmarshes are fertile feeding grounds for birds, especially the mudflats of river estuaries. Here, millions of worms and shellfish live in the rich silt.

The main danger to these wet areas is drainage, for this destroys them completely. Saltmarshes, especially estuaries, are being cleared by dredgers to make room for more and bigger ships. Wetland soil is often rich and makes good farmland once it is drained. As farmers try to grow the maximum amount of food, they are even draining small muddy patches.

The rich mud of saltmarshes feeds thousands of wading birds. Every winter, about three million waders come to feed on Britain's saltmarshes. These include knots, and grey and golden plover, as well as the native dunlin, curlew and redshank.

The Norfolk Broads were made in medieval times when people dug out peat from the marsh. The holes they left filled with water. Today, the Broads are a lovely place to go sailing, and have become a popular holiday area. At least this means that they will probably not be destroyed by draining, but there is another danger. Whether plants and animals can actually survive there depends on our care. We must be careful not to pollute the environment with oil from boats or chemicals.

Bogs consist mostly of peat, which is very acid. Moss is the most common plant. The few leafy plants have special ways of coping with the problem of getting food from acid water. Many, like this sundew, obtain protein by catching and digesting insects.

A few hundred years ago, there were vast areas of wet reedbeds in East Anglia. Now many have been drained for farming. Some of the remaining few have been turned into nature reserves. This means that odd corners of land are saved for shy fen creatures like this rare marsh warbler. Other birds have been saved by nature reserves. They include Savi's warbler, the sedge and reed warblers, and bigger birds like the heron, bittern, and the marsh harrier which now breeds in East Anglia.

Upland

The highest land is bare mountain where just a few hardy little plants can grow. Below this, there may be evergreen forest or boggy heath. The Scottish moors are very boggy and covered with wet moss.

In the past, most damage to highlands was done by people who shot grouse for sport. They killed anything which might kill the grouse first! They also burned off the heather to make fresh sprouts grow to provide food for the grouse. This destroyed other wildlife that lived among the heather. Today there is another danger. More land is needed for crops, livestock and for planting trees. As a result, more and more of the wild upland is being lost.

Some of the wildest places in Britain are in the Highlands of Scotland. It is hard to farm the land here, which is often boggy or rocky, with bitter winters. Now, modern methods, together with necessity, are taming even the Highlands.

About a quarter of Europe's golden eagles live in Scotland. These magnificent birds are still hunted by farmers, game-keepers and egg-collectors, even though this is forbidden by law. Many farmers and keepers believe that golden eagles are a danger to the animals in their care. In fact, they mostly eat rabbits, rodents and occasionally some carrion. They rarely hurt livestock.

High moors on southern uplands are a result of farming by prehistoric people. They chose sandy soil because it was easy to dig and gave good crops for a few years. When the land was exhausted, the farmers moved on to new land, leaving behind poor soil which would only grow bracken and heather. Gradually this man-made habitat evolved a system of wildlife all its own.

Mountain pine forests give food and shelter to a different collection of plants and animals – but mostly animals. This is because evergreen trees take too much light for most undergrowth to survive beneath them. Pine martens like this one hunt in the branches of the trees.

Woodland

If the population of northern Europe were to disappear, nearly the whole of the land would return to forest. Only the tops of mountains, coasts and wetlands would remain almost treeless. Once, two-thirds of Britain was covered in forest. Now, less than a tenth of the land has trees growing on it. In fact, woodland life is the most ancient wildlife of northern Europe. The badgers, foxes, deer and mice that remain in the woods once shared their home with wild boar, wolves and bears. Forest birds like owls, woodpeckers, jays, nuthatches and treecreepers were also much more common in the past. Oak, beech, ash, pine and mixed woodland all grow in different ways. The soil, the weather, and what man has done in the past, all determine how the wood will grow. In an old wood, there may be bluebells and wood anemones. Where the air is clean, different lichens grow on the tree trunks. When it is left alone, a wood is a very rich habitat indeed.

For hundreds of years, our woodlands have given timber for building and fuel. This does not mean that the woods themselves were destroyed. Timber can be taken without killing a tree by a method much used by foresters of the past. They cut a tree so that it would give more wood by 'coppicing', a technique which made many tall, straight trunks grow from one tree. You can still find old coppiced woodland in many parts of Britain. But as the demand for timber grows, machinery is used to speed up the process. Modern machinery makes coppicing difficult and expensive. Slow-growing trees likes oaks are often replaced by faster-growing pines. This is fine for pine-forest creatures, but it can mean death and destruction for the much richer life of mixed and deciduous woodland.

Wood anemones only live where trees have grown since the days of the medieval 'wildwood'. Other plants of ancient woodland are sweet woodruff, yellow pimpernel and wild lily-of-the-valley.

Bracket fungus

Dog's mercury

Common shrew

Woodrush

Bank vole

Woodants

Badgers are among the largest creatures left in our woods. A serious threat has come from the discovery that badgers may carry tuberculosis. This is a disease that causes cows to give milk which is dangerous to drink. Some people think the answer is to kill all badgers. Others say this will not work. While they argue about how to deal with the problem, many badgers are being killed.

Great spotted woodpecker

Elm

Oak

Hazel

Crumble cap

Nightingales like old coppiced woodland. Regular coppicing helps many plants and animals because it lets in light and this allows the undergrowth beneath to flourish.

Ivy

Scarlet cups

Bluebells

Stinkhorn

Longicorn beetle

Witches' butter

Fly-agaric

Woodmouse

Snail

As old mixed woods like this are cut down, they are being replaced by fast-growing evergreen trees. These are set in straight lines so that machines can easily pass between the rows. Evergreen woods are dark places and do not support the variety of wildlife of old mixed woodland. In real life, you would not find all these plants out at the same time of year.

Trees

Not all trees grow in woods. Some trees are found in meadow-land, where they may have been planted long ago to improve the view from a country house or to give shade to cattle. They may also have grown from ancient hedges. Trees in open country are vitally important for wildlife. Insects hiding in the bark, and nuts and seeds like acorns and beechmast provide food for birds and other creatures such as mice, voles and squirrels. A solitary tree may be an oasis for wildlife in a desert of farmland.

The problem is that most farmers try to grow the maximum amount of grain on their fields. For them, trees waste space. Where the tree casts its small patch of shade, crops do not grow so well. Trees get in the way of farm machinery, too. Once a tree has died or been cut down, it is often not replaced. The loss of trees from farmland was a threat to wildlife before the killer Dutch elm disease came to Britain.

We will probably lose nearly all our elms to this disease. Now, even more than before, every tree deliberately cut down or damaged is a tragedy for wildlife.

The oak is so much part of the landscape that we may not notice how much rarer it is becoming. Oaks are slow-growing trees, so the faster-growing conifers are planted instead. Oaks probably support more wildlife than any other tree. For instance, 190 different species of moth caterpillars eat oak leaves.

Left: Rooks feed in open country. They like grubs that live in the ground, such as leather-jackets and wireworms, and are very much at home on farmland. They are social birds and nest in groups in a clump of trees. Unfortunately, their favourite trees are elms, and they will be affected by the spread of Dutch elm disease.

Above: Blue tits feed on the little insects that hide in tree bark. They nest in holes in trees, often choosing elms.

Above: Dutch elm disease came from Canada less than 20 years ago. It arrived in some logs, and has spread so quickly that over 17 million out of the 23 million elms in southern England are already dead.

Left: The disease is caused by a fungus carried by elm bark beetles. They lay their eggs under the bark and the grubs feed on the tree. The next year, they emerge as beetles and fly off to infect more trees.

Heathland

Most southern heathland is man-made. Heath soil is nearly always sandy, which gives us a clue to its history. Stone Age people found sandy soil easiest to dig. They cut down trees on sandy soil, let their pigs clear the undergrowth, and grew crops there until the land was exhausted. Then they moved on to another patch of sandy woodland. Later, heathland was used for grazing cattle and sheep, and the Normans kept their rabbits on it. The heath was kept open by burning. This got rid of heather and made new green sprouts grow.

Although heath is not completely natural, it has been with us for so long that a wide variety of plants and animals are adapted to make use of it. One of the strangest examples is a moth whose caterpillar feeds on a fungus that only grows on burnt gorse and birch twigs, so the moth actually depends on regular burning of heath.

Many heaths are being lost to sand and gravel workings. Others are being planted with trees. Those that remain have been turned into nature reserves or golf courses and are visited by large numbers of people. Even though heathland depends on fire for its existence, fire is also a great danger. A fire in early summer can destroy a heath so thoroughly that it may be half a century before it grows back again. This is because when the shallow soil is dry, fire burns right through the top peaty layer, killing the roots of grasses, heather and gorse. A fire can easily be started by a carelessly dropped cigarette or match, and may smoulder for days before a breeze fans it into flame. You will see racks of brooms on many heaths. They are fire-beaters and should be used immediately by anyone who sees smoke.

Many heathland birds lay their eggs on the ground. They are usually well camouflaged like these whimbrel eggs. A spring fire is disastrous for the young.

Below: Dunwich heath is a nature reserve and people can enjoy its wild scenery whenever they like. Although it is cared for by the National Trust, its safety depends on the care that its visitors take if it is to survive.

Nightjars have suffered badly from the loss of heathland. They nest among the heather, but they feed on the larger insects from nearby woodland.

Lizards are becoming more rare. The common lizard, above, is still the most common. Sand lizards and slow-worms are now very rare indeed. When the common lizard lays its eggs, they are ready to hatch. The babies can hunt for themselves almost immediately.

The number of Dartford warblers in Britain has recently increased to over 100 pairs. This is almost entirely due to careful management of heathland nature reserves. These birds need open heathland with plenty of heather. They also like a gorse bush to use as a song-post. Without protection, Dartford warblers would die out.

Farmland

For 3,000 years, man has been clearing forests, tilling fields, keeping animals, and working hard to get as much as possible out of the land. Farmland is not a truly natural habitat, but it is the biggest one we have. A host of plants and animals depend on it for their living.

Farmland belongs to the farmers, and they control most of the countryside. Until about 30 years ago, many farms looked like the one in the picture. Now, the real threat to wildlife on farmland is the growing population. Most of us live in towns. We do not ourselves go out and drive our cars over meadows, or stamp on wild plants. But we do ask farmers to grow more and more food as cheaply as possible. The machines farmers use to do this work best on big fields full of single crops. But with a big field, a pest or disease can spread like wildfire, and this means disaster for the farmer. So he uses poisons, not to cure disease but to prevent it.

Every year the pests and diseases become harder to kill and the farmers use more poisons and chemicals. It is the wildlife of the countryside that suffers most in this war. If we want to save the countryside, new ways must be found to grow and harvest crops which do not need such powerful poisons to keep them healthy.

Ladybirds eat huge quantities of aphids. But wherever aphids are poisoned by insecticides, ladybirds are poisoned too. Unfortunately, the next year the aphids come back in even greater numbers. The ladybirds take longer to recover.

Key:
1 Teasel
2 Blackberries
3 Great burnet
4 Hedge woundwort
5 Yarrow
6 Lady's mantle
7 Hogweed
8 Red campion
9 Dog violet
10 Old man's beard
11 Ivy
12 Apple orchard

In the past, most farmers grew crops and raised livestock. They controlled pests and weeds by crop rotation. Instead of expensive chemical fertilizers, they used the manure from their animals. Traditional methods like these do less damage to wildlife.

Colorado beetles are one of the potato farmer's deadliest enemies. A big field of just one crop is always at the mercy of fast-breeding pests like this. One solution is to use poisons. Another solution might be to grow mixed crops. But these are much more difficult to harvest. Most farmers will not spend the extra time.

Hedgerows

When hedgerows were planted, they were simply a way of enclosing fields to stop livestock straying. They were also a cheap and easy way of marking a boundary which could not easily be moved. But hedgerows are not just a pretty part of the landscape. Now that woodland is so scarce, they are specially important. About ten million birds nest in Britain's hedges, and the number of small mammals which make their homes in or under hedges is probably even greater. Hundreds of plants grow in or near hedgerows. Often, hedges have a sunny and a shady side, each growing different plants. A hedge is also an important nursery for young trees. Many great oaks and elms began as sprouts in an ancient hedgerow. The hedgerows of Britain join the whole country together in a network of stretched-out woodland. This enables animals to move around freely under cover.

Hedgerows are not just threatened, they are under attack. Between 1946 and 1963, 136,000 kilometres of hedgerow were destroyed in Britain, at a rate of 8,000 kilometres a year! The fact is that many farmers prefer not to have hedges. They get in the way of machinery and take up valuable space. But, apart from providing homes for wildlife, hedges help prevent soil from blowing away. The bees and insects that live in them pollinate crops, and hedgerow birds eat insect pests. Today, farmers usually trim hedges with flailing machines. This kills many young saplings.

Nowadays, many farmers prefer an electric fence to a hedge. It needs next to no maintenance, and can be quickly moved. But a hedge can give shelter from sun and wind. It provides food for many animals, as well as colour and beauty in autumn.

Hedges are not the only natural way of dividing fields. In places where stone is plentiful, it has long been used to keep sheep and cattle from straying. Stone soon gets covered by a crop of lichens, and all kinds of rock plants which bees and butterflies especially like to feed on. Lichens only grow well where the air is clean.

This mixed hedgerow is the home of many plants and animals. Here, a wren, guarding its territory, keeps a watchful eye on a pair of dunnocks and a hungry woodmouse.

You can work out roughly how old a hedge is by counting the number of different kinds of woody plants in it. The number in a 27-metre stretch gives you the hedge's approximate age in centuries. The older the hedge is, the more creatures it shelters.

Dangers Introduced

Once, some animals and plants were confined to certain parts of the world. The only way they could invade new territory was when great geological changes occurred. Man now moves animals and plants from country to country. Sometimes the results are bad for the countryside and ourselves. Black rats, which came to London in sailing ships, caused the Great Plague of 1665. The Normans took rabbits with them to Britain, which helped prevent trees growing back on heathland.

Most exotic animals and plants can only survive in zoos, but occasionally one manages to make itself at home. There are now 42 'foreign' species of animal living happily in the wild in Britain, including wallabies. Dutch elm disease is a recent arrival from abroad, too. But perhaps the worst threat is the killer disease, rabies. It attacks carnivorous animals and human beings. It does not exist in Britain yet, but it is just across the English Channel. Pets must not be brought in without quarantine.

The mink is a carnivore related to martens and weasels. Wild minks live along rivers all over Europe but, until 1924, there were none in Britain. Then some American minks were brought here to breed for fur. A few escaped and found the waters of Britain much to their liking. They have no natural enemies, and are fierce little

American grey squirrels arrived here between 1876 and 1920. They are bigger and stronger than the native red squirrels, which they have now driven almost to extinction. These new-comers are a pest in evergreen forests. They strip bark off trees, and prey on birds and eggs.

hunters themselves. Some people think they are a threat to the native wildlife, but we do not yet know enough about how they live to be sure.

Another animal first brought to Britain for fur breeding is the coypu. Its fur is called nutria. Like the mink, it lives in wet places. Coypus are large rodents – they look like guinea pigs and are about 60 cm long. When they escaped, they found the fenlands comfortable. They dug big holes in river-banks, ate reeds and even damaged farmland. Steps are being taken to exterminate them.

About 15 years ago, this European fish was brought to the fens to make fishing more interesting. It is a zander, a relation of the perch. Zanders are fierce hunters. By 1978, they had eaten nine-tenths of all other fish in the River Ouse. The angling societies are now trying desperately to stop zanders spreading to other rivers. They are catching as many as possible to try to save the other fish. This is an example of how even the experts can make mistakes that seriously affect our wildlife.

Hunting

Before man the farmer, there was man the hunter. The need to kill seems to be very strong in some people, though most people no longer have to hunt to survive.

Many hunted animals have no value at all as food. Elephants are killed for their ivory tusks. Big cats and snakes are killed for their skins, although it is now illegal to use the skins of some endangered animals. It is not only in the jungles of the world that animals are killed for no useful purpose. In Britain, many people enjoy hunting for sport, some legally, and many illegally.

Illegal traps are among the cruellest things in the countryside. Although gin traps and snares were banned by law years ago, many wild animals, not to mention pet cats and dogs, are horribly injured by them. Animals protected by law are also being shot. Many gamekeepers regard birds of prey as a threat to the creatures in their care. They sometimes even shoot owls, though any damage they do to young game birds is probably outweighed by the service they perform in catching rats. Unfortunately, it is hard to catch people who break the law in this way because they usually leave no evidence of their guilt.

Killing animals by poisoning is illegal, but the use of poisons such as strychnine is increasing. The only way this can be stopped is by making sure the culprits are caught and punished. Sadly, though, not all the unnecessary killing man does is illegal.

Above: Seals eat the same fish that we want to eat. This is given as the reason why thousands of baby seals are killed every year. It is unlikely that seals do as much damage to fisheries as is caused by illegal fishing methods.

Most of Britain's wild birds are protected by law. It is even illegal to go near the nests of many species. But this is not the case throughout Europe. Every year, up to 150 million birds are shot as they fly south to Africa for the winter. Some of these, like this little garden warbler, breed in our countryside. This means that our protection is particularly important.

In a few years, whales may have been hunted to extinction. If the whaling industry continues the slaughter, it too will become extinct. However, some countries refuse to stop killing whales.

The buzzard lives in hilly, wooded country, catching mice, rats, rabbits, birds and insects. Like other birds of prey, buzzards are now protected and it is illegal to kill them or take their eggs. But they are easy to spot and often become a target for hunters.

Left: Some farmers and gamekeepers inject poison like strychnine into a dead rabbit or an egg. This is then left out for any bird or animal that comes along. The use of poisons like this is illegal. Many of the animals killed are protected species. Between 1975 and 1978 over 200 protected animals died in Britain by poisoning, including nine golden eagles and a rare marsh harrier.

Air Pollution

There is one danger to the countryside which is a threat to every part of it. This is the pollution of the air that all living things must breathe.

Wherever we live we burn things, both in industry and at home. The smoke from burning petrol, factory chimneys and fires is not just dirty. It carries all kinds of poisons into the air. If they go high in the air, these poisons can travel around the world. In Scandinavia, rain is turned into acid by sulphurous fumes from Britain's factories.

It is not just the outpourings of factories that poison the air. We add a little bit more pollution every time we use an aerosol can. Nobody is quite sure what damage aerosols are doing, but it might be safer to do without them.

Lichens are a good guide to how clean the air is. Some are so sensitive that they only grow where the air is absolutely pure. In fairly dirty air, you can find crusty lichens on trees and rocks. Leafy lichens grow in cleaner air. The shrubby ones that look like tangled, dried seaweed only grow in the cleanest air. Lungwort needs the cleanest air and it is only found in old, undisturbed forest.

Above: Epping Forest is just outside London, and plenty of dirty London air reaches it. Here, in the last 200 years, 90 species of lichen have died out. This is not because of the people that visit the forest. It is because the lichens breathe the same polluted air.

The exhaust fumes from burnt petrol add many different poisons to the air. One is carbon monoxide which can kill quickly if it escapes in a confined space. Lead, which causes damage and kills slowly, also builds up to dangerously high levels in towns.

Factory chimneys are made tall to take smoke high up into the air. This carries it away from the factory buildings. Instead, it travels in air currents all over the countryside – sometimes all over the world. Factory smoke may contain a number of things which in large enough quantities can be dangerous to life. They include lead, mercury, zinc, copper, arsenic and sulphur.

Into Extinction

The climate of Europe has varied a great deal in the history of the world. It has been much warmer than it is now, and much colder. The last Ice Age lasted for two million years, and only ended fifteen thousand years ago. It killed many insects, reptiles and amphibians. Mammoths, bears, reindeer, beavers, wolves and wild boars managed to survive the Ice Age but none of them live in Britain now. Some animals, like mammoths and reindeer, were so well adapted to the cold that they could not live in the new forests which grew when the ice melted. Some managed to adapt to the forests but could not survive being hunted, for Stone Age people also lived in Europe through most of the Ice Age.

The big forest creatures are now gone. Today, much of the wildlife in Europe lives on farmland. The question is, can this wildlife survive our modern farming methods?

Below: Mammoths lived in northern Europe during the Ice Age. They probably became extinct when the ice melted, because the open spaces they needed to feed on became overgrown with forest. Possibly, mammoths were helped into extinction by Stone Age hunters.

Left: The large blue butterfly has a strange life-cycle. The caterpillars first feed on wild thyme and later on the grubs of red ants. Large blues are now extinct in Britain. In 1979 the last remaining colony failed to breed.

Right: The last wolf in Britain died about 250 years ago. Wolves survived the Ice Age and were still common when the Romans came. But the forests became smaller and smaller and wolves were relentlessly hunted until they were exterminated. They were hunted mainly out of fear, as is still the case in the parts of Europe where they live now.

Left: The Irish elk was a huge animal. It had the biggest antlers of any deer that has ever lived. Its large size helped to keep it warm through the Ice Age, but we do not know why it had such big antlers. Deer shed their antlers every year, so a good deal of food must have been wasted in growing them. Perhaps this was one reason why the elk became extinct when the Ice Age ended.

Above: Sabretooths were big cats with extremely long upper canine teeth. They probably used them to slash through the thick hide of Ice Age elephants. Sabretooths became extinct at the same time as their prey. They were so well adapted to this method of hunting they could not live in any other way.

Above left: Brown bears still live in Europe. They existed in Scotland until about 1,000 years ago. Like wolves they were killed through fear. When people are afraid of something, they often kill it to show their courage. Today, we have no cause to fear the wild.

Just Surviving

Many plants and animals are on the edge of extinction. This tells us that the world of nature – our world – is not in balance. Every species lost can never be regained.

Farmers and gardeners know that they need a wide variety of different plants and animals from which to breed new and better sheep, cattle, chickens and plant crops. They have now begun to keep stocks of seeds and 'old-fashioned' animals to make sure they will not die out. The world as a whole needs to keep its variety of life. It is natural for some species to die out as time goes by, of course. But the rate at which this is happening now is not natural – it is caused by man.

The animals and plants shown here are only a few of the great number of species which are dying. Some species are now recognized as being endangered, but they are not always the rarest ones. The very rarest may not yet have been discovered. They could be dying out before we know about them.

Yellow archangel does not survive being dug up or disturbed. It only grows in old woods – the type called primary wood. This means that the woods have existed for thousands of years. Primary woodlands grow many more kinds of plants than the newer secondary woods, but they are becoming much scarcer.

The osprey was once common in Scotland, but it was hunted to such a degree that, between 1916 and 1955, not a single osprey nested in Britain. Now ospreys are back in Scotland. The first successful pair raised three chicks in 1959. The birds still have to be guarded during the breeding season to protect them from people who would steal the eggs and chicks to sell them to collectors. Disturbing any nesting bird, or stealing the young is, of course, against the law.

Horseshoe bats are now a protected species. Bats have a hard time in winter in northern Europe. They must sleep very deeply, to make their stores of fat last until the warm weather brings back insects for them to eat. If they are disturbed, they may die of starvation before the spring.

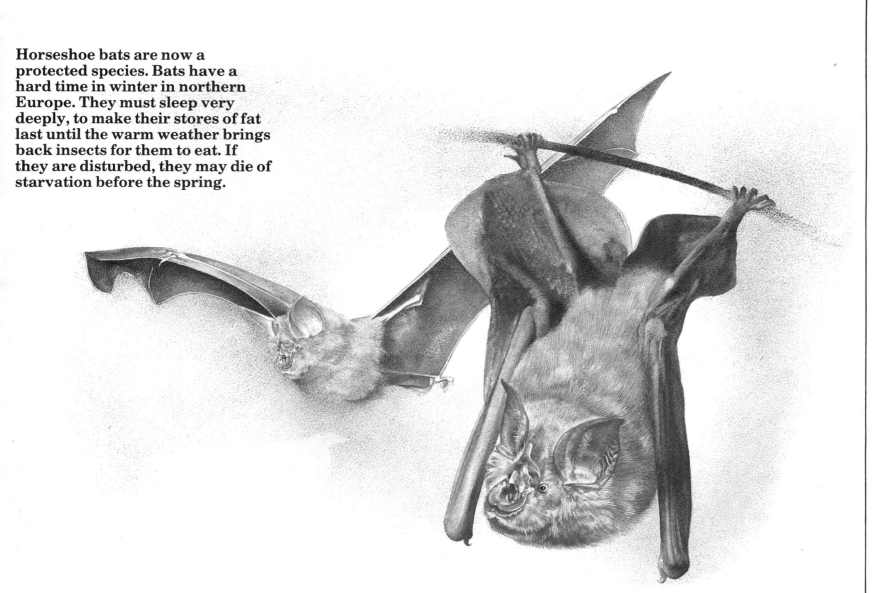

Every part of the world has its wild cats. As a family, cats are the most successful hunters in the world. There is only one kind of wild cat in Britain. Our wild cats are moorland creatures, though they sometimes live in woods. They have been hunted for hundreds of years, but still survive on the Scottish moors.

Peregrine falcons have suffered badly from pesticides. They eat pigeons which feed on farmland which is often treated with chemicals. These poisons cause the falcons to lay thin-shelled eggs which break before they hatch.

Protected Animals

Otters are among Britain's largest wild animals. Like any other wild animal they are only protected when they are in grave danger of extinction. In 1980, otters were considered to be a common breed and they were legally hunted for sport. The following year, they were so rare that they were protected. In a few years, there may be enough otters for them to be hunted again.

It is hard to help animals to survive in the wild. What they really need is space and peace. Unfortunately, people often want the land where the animals have made their home. In the last few years, however, it has been decided to help some animals by making laws to protect them.

One law forbids anyone to kill very rare creatures or deliberately to interfere with them. Even scientists who study them have to get special permission and a licence. To start with, the laws protecting animals did not include their habitats. Very recently, however, there have been new EEC rules and a new British law called the Wildlife and Countryside Act 1981, which help to protect special habitats.

Besides the animals shown here, nearly all the birds in Britain are protected by law, at least when they are breeding. Bats have been given special protection, too. The rarest are the mouse-eared bat and the greater horseshoe bat. These bats hibernate in caves in the winter, and one reason why they have become rare is that there are fewer places for them to hibernate safely. Even being disturbed by the scientists studying them may be enough to tip the balance against their survival. But scientists have also been finding out how to help them, so there is some hope for these mysterious little creatures of the night.

Three kinds of snail and two spiders have recently been given protection. A single fish, the burbot, has also been put on the list of protected animals. But it may be too late to save the burbot. Nobody has caught one in Britain for at least 12 years.

We can help all animals, whether they are officially protected or not, by treating them with respect. Then perhaps laws will no longer be needed to help creatures in trouble.

We are used to thinking of insects as troublemakers, but now 14 insects are protected in Britain – a beetle, a dragonfly, two crickets, a grasshopper, four butterflies and five moths. The Essex emerald moth, shown here, lives only on Essex saltmarshes, where its caterpillars eat sea wormwood.

The natterjack toad has very short legs and cannot hop at all, but it can run very fast in short bursts. It is a dry-land creature and lives in sandy places but it must have water to breed. It is the rarest of our amphibians, but the others may soon become just as rare.

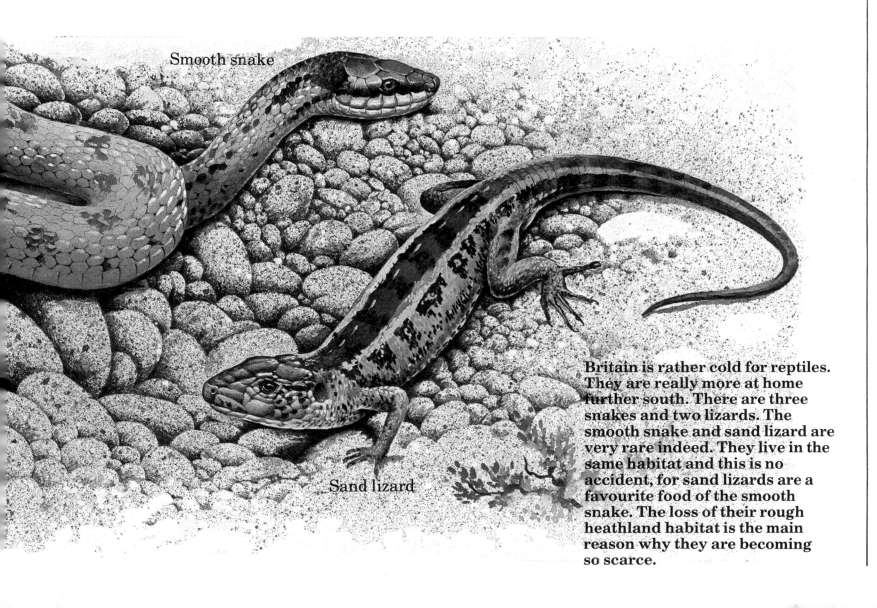

Smooth snake

Sand lizard

Britain is rather cold for reptiles. They are really more at home further south. There are three snakes and two lizards. The smooth snake and sand lizard are very rare indeed. They live in the same habitat and this is no accident, for sand lizards are a favourite food of the smooth snake. The loss of their rough heathland habitat is the main reason why they are becoming so scarce.

Protected Plants

There are 61 plants in Britain which are protected by law. This makes it illegal for anyone to pick, dig up or kill them. It is also illegal to dig up any wild plant without good reason. When a protected plant grows by a roadside, it may be marked by a white post. When the verge is cut, the blade of the machine is raised to avoid the plant.

As well as being endangered by pollution and other disturbances to their habitat, plants suffer from well-meaning people. There are many ways of studying and enjoying plants without hurting them. We can draw or photograph them instead of picking or pressing them. If we leave them alone, other people can enjoy them too. Even quite ordinary plants can become rare very quickly if they are picked before they have a chance to make new seeds. Once, cowslips were so common that people picked bowls full of the flower-heads to make wine. Now cowslips are very rare. To a scientist, a flower is most interesting when in its proper place. He wants to know where it lives and how it grows – things a picked flower cannot tell him.

The rare lady's slipper orchid is one of our loveliest plants. Most orchids have smaller flowers, many of them drab, but this one is large and bright. It grows on limestone hills, flowering early in the summer. It was once widespread, but has been dug up by collectors so it can now only be found in one place in Britain.

There are a number of gentians in Europe. About eight different kinds live in Britain, but four are now rare. Two are protected – the spring gentian and the smaller Alpine gentian. Both grow in stony places on hills. Gentians are not the rarest plants in Britain, but they have always been rather special because they look so delicate while growing in such unfriendly places. Spring gentian is a perennial but Alpine is an annual, which means it must make new seeds every year to survive.

This pretty little evergreen plant is called diapensia. It is another protected mountain plant. Diapensia really belongs to the tundra, much further north than Britain, but it has probably been here since the Ice Age. It just manages to survive in a few places, like many of our rare plants.

The wild gladiolus is related to the iris. It grows in marshy places and scrubby heathland, but the true wild gladiolus is difficult to find. Its cultivated relation sometimes spreads from gardens and also look as if it is growing wild.

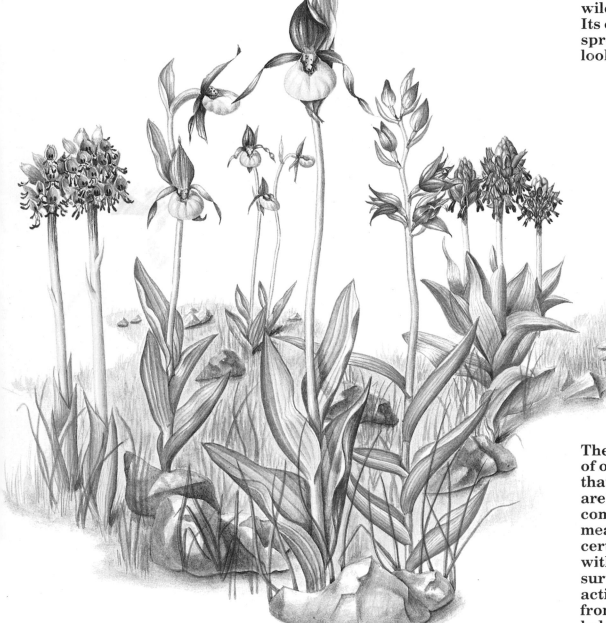

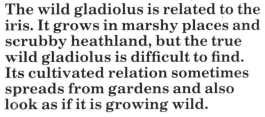

There are seven protected species of orchids, out of over 50 species that grow in Britain. At least ten are rare. Most orchids have a complicated life cycle, which means that they can only grow in certain places. Never interfere with any orchid. They will not survive being transplanted. Even actions like trying to save them from being ploughed up will not help them.

How You Can Help

There are many ways you can help the wild to survive. If you have a garden, start by helping the birds. Never put out white bread or salty food, however. Try to find out what they eat naturally, and give them something similar. Once you begin to feed them, of course, you must carry on until the spring – they will come to depend on your help.

You could make a small pond in even a tiny garden. Dig a shallow hole and line it with strong plastic sheeting. Fill it with rain-water, put a little soil in the water and try to get a jar of water, mud and weed from a natural pond.

Not everyone has a garden. But everybody can help clear up the countryside by keeping it clear of rubbish. You could take a strong plastic bag with you to the country or seaside, to collect any rubbish you find. You will be surprised at the strange things that turn up. (Be careful if you find old light bulbs – they may explode if you pick them up with warm hands). Put the rubbish in a litter-bin.

It is very easy to make a bird-table, if you want to feed birds. Make sure your bird-table keeps birds safe from cats. Put it on a post so that even if a cat climbs up it cannot get on top. A roof is not essential but it helps to keep food dry and free of snow. You can also hang up scraps of fat in plastic nets.

Insects such as bees, butterflies and moths, as well as many flies feed on the nectar of flowers. Buddleia flowers are among their favourites, and planting a buddleia bush will attract some beautiful butterflies. Attracting insects helps everything in the garden. It provides birds with natural food and will encourage them to nest near you. It attracts bees which pollinate your fruit and vegetables. You can help even more by not using poisons in your garden to kill pests.

A small untidy corner of the garden can be a haven for wildlife. Try making a bat-box. It should be like a bird's nesting-box but with a slit entrance near the bottom, instead of a round entrance near the top. Bats cannot hibernate in it, but it will help them to breed. Attach it to a sturdy tree or quiet wall.

Leaving ordinary rubbish around like this adds to the general pollution problem. But, unlike the pollution from industry, it is very easy to prevent. You can help by picking up rubbish wherever you find it and getting rid of it properly. Another way you can help is by not buying things which are over-wrapped. Double wrapping means double litter, and it also uses up twice as much wood, oil and fuel to make the wrapping. Everyone can help prevent waste in small ways.

Conservation

There is a lot you can do alone, but even more when you get together with other people. A number of organizations which care for the countryside have junior branches. The Royal Society for the Protection of Birds (RSPB) has a very active junior club called the Young Ornithologists Club (YOC). It costs very little to join, and you get regular magazines, competitions and a chance to meet other young bird-watchers. The Royal Society for Nature Conservation has a busy junior section called WATCH. Their addresses are: YOC, The Lodge, Sandy, Bedfordshire. WATCH, The Green, Nettleham, Lincoln.

Toads travel the same way to their breeding ponds every year. When a road is built across their path, hundreds of toads get run over. A little care from motorists could save them.

This pond is a disgrace. The water has become stagnant and dead, and now only a scum of red algae grows in it. Pollution may be the cause of this mess but, with proper treatment, it can be made into an attractive place again.

A healthy pond is a lovely place to be near. More than that, it is a home for many of the water creatures which are suffering so badly from neglected, polluted or drained ponds. Perhaps the best chance for these creatures is in restored town and village ponds like this.

It is sometimes difficult to persuade badgers to use tunnels specially built for them to cross roads safely. They use the same paths for years, one generation after another, and are very much at risk from cars.

Keeping foothpaths open helps people to see the countryside without causing damage. If paths are clear, people use them instead of breaking through hedges. County Conservation Trusts help keep footpaths clear.

Ringed plover

Gull

Sandpiper

Oyster catcher

Redshank

Lapwing

Ruff

Using a hide allows you to look at birds without disturbing them. This kind of hide is built by the RSPB so that anyone can watch birds on their reserves. The birds get used to the building and they cannot see the people inside, so you can watch them behaving normally. A pair of binoculars will help you to see even better.

Hope in Towns

The best hope for wildlife may be in towns. This is not as unlikely as it may sound. Apart from pollution, many problems facing wildlife do not exist in towns. We do not grow crops in towns, so some of the farmer's weeds can grow there without bothering anyone. Waste ground can grow thistles, dock, poppies, willowherb, and all the grasses the farmer hates to see.

All kinds of wildlife already live in and around towns. Pigeons nest on buildings right in the middle of big cities, as their ancestors once nested on cliffs. Pied wagtails roost on factory roofs. Black redstarts nest on power stations, and even kestrels nest on high buildings. Even more creatures are found in parks and gardens. Frogs and toads may depend completely on garden ponds for survival. Magpies, kestrels, hedgehogs, squirrels and foxes all appear in town gardens from time to time.

In 1957, the River Thames was so badly polluted by sewage that the water contained almost no oxygen for 72 kilometres downstream of London. There were no fishes living in this murky water, nor much of anything else. Then a new way of treating sewage before it went into the river was tried. The River Thames came back to life, its oxygen returned, and fish came back one by one. Now, even a salmon is thought to have swum through to London without suffocating.

You can now find foxes in towns. This one was photographed as it came to see what it could find in a dustbin. In some places, foxes have even managed to raise a family in town gardens.

Rock plants can grow well on city walls as long as they can stand the polluted air. This plant is a stone-crop called navelwort. It lives naturally on rocks where there is no lime, so the acid air of a city might suit it well. Church-yards are good places where plants, especially rock plants, can grow, undisturbed by people.

This station wall is growing a good sheet of creeper. Railways generally are a haven for wildlife. They form a network all over the country, where grass is not cut. Young trees often get a good start on railway embankments, and many shy creatures get quite used to trains rushing by while they raise their families.

Here is a hopeful sight. A young tawny owl waits in a flowering cherry tree for its parents to bring food after dark. Many creatures could find homes in our gardens.

All we have to do is let a few trees grow thick, provide a nest-box or two, and cut down on the amount of killer chemicals that we use. For, in the end, a world without

garden pests means a world without most birds too. The wild is surely more valuable to us than being able to cultivate a perfect rose.

Index

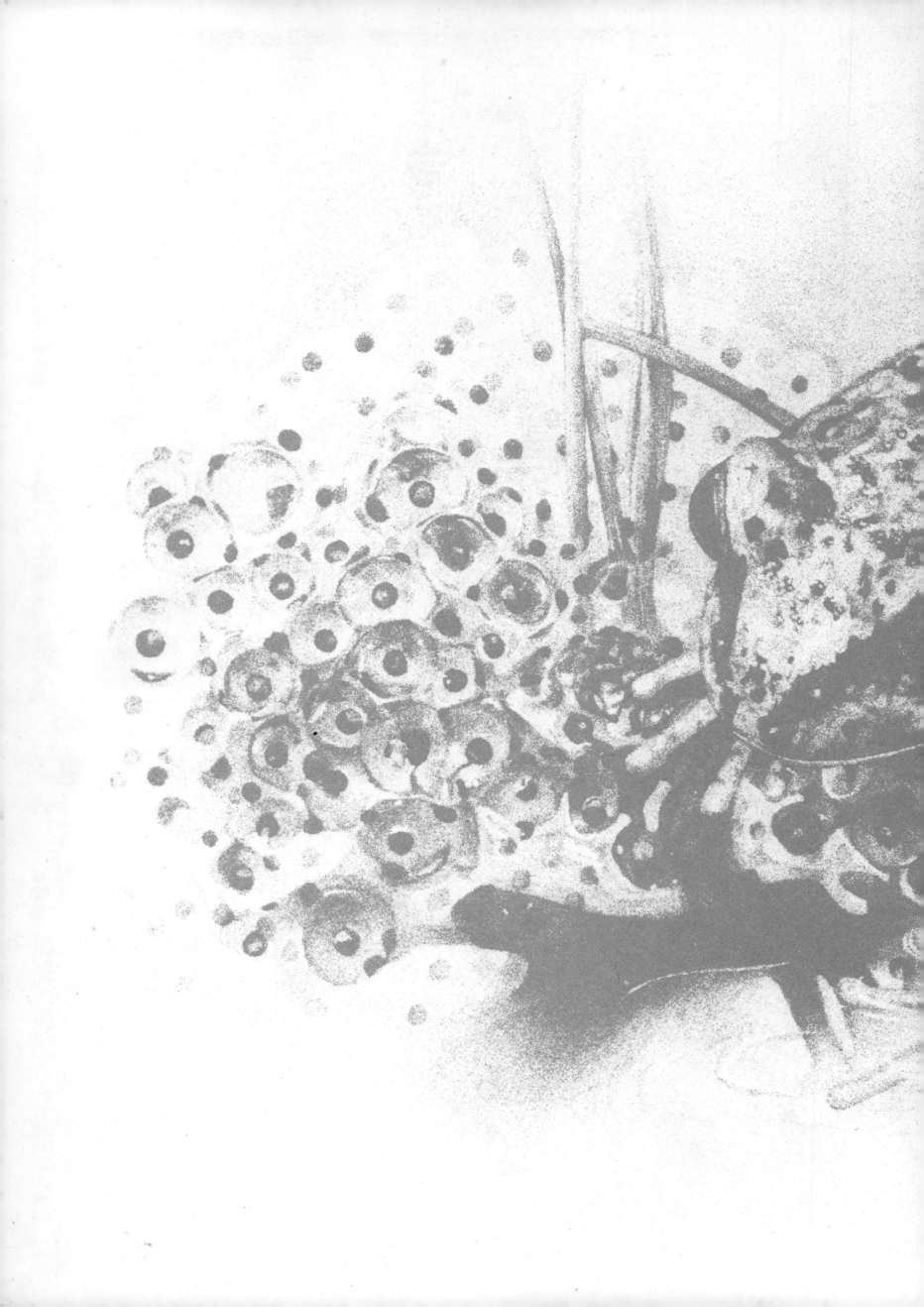